St Mary's Hall

Guide to the Building its History ıd Contents

y Joan C. Lancaster CBE FSA
rawings by Robert Overy FRSA

R. OVERY. 79

he Coventry Papers No. 3

xterior from Bayley Lane

First published 1948 by the City of Coventry
2nd edition 1981

ISBN 0-901606-65-0

City of Coventry 1981

Preface

It is now over thirty years since the first *Guide to St Mary's Hall* was issued in 1948. Meanwhile, others have studied the building, have written about it and have asked questions. Not the least of the questioners have been the part-time Guides whom I was privileged to meet during several lengthy visits in October 1979. Although there was still much work to be done on the building, I was once more moved by its splendour and its agelessness. The nineteenth-century antiquaries were right in their enthusiasm for this treasure house, which does indeed merit full-scale protection and preservation for both present and future generations.

The first edition owed much to the local knowledge of Mr (later Sir) Charles Barratt, then Town Clerk, Mr E H Ford, then City Engineer, Mr Philip Chatwin, Mr (now Dr) Levi Fox, Mr Frederick Smith, Mr S C Kaines Smith, Mr William Storer and Mr J B Shelton; and to the advice on the portraits of Sir Henry Hake and Mr G K Adams, then of the National Portrait Gallery.

For this second edition it seemed right, while revising the existing text, to re-cast the historical as well as the descriptive parts of it. My recent research has enabled me to make fuller use of the illuminating work of the antiquaries William Reader, Thomas Sharp and W G Fretton, and to benefit from later studies by: Professor Pevsner and Mrs Wedgwood (Buildings of England, 1966); Mrs Margaret Tomlinson (architectural adviser to the Victoria County Histories, 1969, her descriptions being based on Mr S R Jones's investigation of 1965); Mr Derek Janes and Mrs Sara Muldoon (Coventry Museum) on various objects in the hall; Mr Patrick Day and Mr R A Clarke (Herbert Art Gallery) on the pictures; Mr S A Wright and Mr P Vyse-Widdicombe (Department of Architecture and Planning) in their detailed survey and plan of St Mary's Hall, the late Mr Reg Trotter (report of 1 May 1979) on the restoration of the roof after war damage; and the Victoria and Albert Museum on the Tapestry. I am grateful to Mr Eric Jackson of the Freemen's Guild for allowing me full access to the north Undercroft, and to Lady Anne Bentinck for permission to quote from Humfrey Wanley's memorandum of 1719 to Lord Harley (in the Portland Papers).

To Mr David Rimmer, the City's Archivist and Editor of the Coventry Papers, and to members of the Civic Affairs Unit I am particularly indebted, and not least for the invitation to undertake this new edition. I owe a special debt of gratitude to Bob Cole (Graphic and Visual Aids Division) for undertaking responsibility for the book and its preparation for the press, to Jan Gould for her expert and imaginative design and layout, and to Chris Jones for his photographs.

For the final paragraph are reserved my warmest appreciation and thanks to Mr Robert Overy, who has devoted to the task of illustrating this new edition the judicious mixture of beauty and accuracy in his drawings, supported by his enthusiasm and historical feeling, which the book required.

Joan C. Lancaster

9 May 1980 **Joan C Lancaster**

eface

Contents

Historical Introduction

Borough and Gild 1
The building of St Mary's Hall 4
Restorations and alterations 8
Feast and function 15

General Description 19

Detailed Description of St Mary's Hall and its Contents 23
Arranged according to the recommended itinerary

The Mercers' Room 25
The Porch 27
The Courtyard 28
The Undercrofts 30
The Cloister (or Lower Lobby) and Main Staircase 32
The Gallery (or Upper Lobby) 33

The Great Hall 34

The Roof 36
The Corbels 37
The East and West Windows 38
The North Window 41
The Tapestry 42
The Dais 46
The Oriel 46
The Portraits 50
The Minstrels' Gallery 51

The Mayoress's Parlour 54
The Drapers' Room 56
The Prince's Chamber 57
The Old Council Chamber 58
The Treasury 63
The Armoury 65
Mary Queen of Scots' Room 66
The Ante Room 67
The Kitchen 68

Appendix 71

List of pictures hanging in St Mary's Hall in 1948 and now in the Herbert Art Gallery

Bibliography 72

Plans 77

Ground floor rooms Plan 1
First floor rooms Plan 2
Second floor rooms Plan 3

Illustrations

[Dr]awings by Robert Overy

St Mary's Hall (Exterior) from Bayley Lane

The Muniment Room 13

Caesar's Tower and the Armoury (from the west) 21

The Porch 28

The Courtyard 29

The main Undercroft (The Crypt) 31

Carved heads at the bottom of the main staircase 32

Angels from the roof of the Great Hall 34

Heraldic bosses from the roof of the Great Hall 36

Corbel in the Great Hall 37

Roundels from the Oriel 46 & 48

Decorated tiles from the Oriel 49

Armour (on the Minstrels' Gallery) 51

The South Window (Great Hall) 53

Scratchings from the windows in the Drapers' Room 56

Wood carvings in the Treasury (from the roof of the Old Council Chamber) 63

St George and the Dragon (Treasury) 64

The Buttery (Armoury) 66

The Ante Room 67

The Kitchen, showing the timber-framed Old Council Chamber 69

Photographs

A page from the Register of the Trinity Gild 3

The Grille between the Kitchen and the Undercroft 16

Arms of the Mercers' Company (Mercers' Room) 24

The Great Hall (Interior) from the south 35

The Great Hall (Interior) from the north 40

The Tapestry 43

The Oriel 47

The Mayoress's Parlour 55

The Prince's Chamber 57

The Old Council Chamber 59

The Gild Chair 60

The Treasury 62

Historical Introduction

ough and Gild

First built between 1340 and 1342 for the merchant gild of St Mary, enlarged between 1394 and 1414 for the united gild (the Trinity Gild) of the Holy Trinity, St Mary the Virgin, St John the Baptist and St Catherine, and extensively altered at the end of the fifteenth century, St Mary's Hall early became the headquarters for the mayor, bailiffs and commonalty after their creation in 1345 by Edward III's charter of incorporation. Borough and gild merchant worked closely together, the Trinity Gild becoming influential in the affairs of the borough, which for its part found it convenient to use the spacious premises of the gild for its deliberations, the reception of royalty and other ceremonial occasions, and may even have played a part in the enlargement of the building in 1394-1414. (It is worth noting here that, while the gild merchant and later the Trinity Gild would appear to have been the chief gild in the earl's half of the town, the Corpus Christi Gild (founded 1348) used St Nicholas Hall in West Orchard and seems to have been the chief gild in the prior's half. The two gilds were however amalgamated in 1534. The division of the town had taken place in the early-twelfth century, the problems inherent in the division not being resolved until after the stormy twenty years or so between 1337 and 1355.)

The gild merchant (a fraternity of brothers and sisters with an elected master), created by charter of Edward III in 1340, was primarily concerned with the regulation of trade in Coventry, but had also religious and ceremonial duties. These and particularly its works of piety were continued by the Trinity Gild which, according to its ordinances, was to support chaplains to perform the daily offices and sing masses in St John's chapel at Bablake for the souls of its benefactors and members; it was to provide financial help for members in need; and it was to observe the feasts of Trinity, the Assumption of the Virgin, St John the Baptist and St Catherine, as well as four anniversaries for departed brothers, sisters and benefactors. At its quarterly meetings in St Mary's Hall, the gild elected its masters and wardens, audited the accounts, leased gild property to tenants, drew up regulations, admitted new members and organised alms-giving, while its observation of feast days soon developed into celebrations of some magnificence.

Within six years of incorporation, the mayor and bailiffs were using St Mary's Hall to collect taxes and in 1355 it was agreed that the mayor should make the town's annual Michaelmas payment of £10 to the prior in the gildhall. The court leet met there to make by-laws governing the economic and social life of the town at Easter, at Michaelmas when the bailiffs were chosen, and on 25 January to elect the mayor and other officers. We may assume that the mayor's council, which first appears in 1421, had already begun to use for its various activities the group of timber-framed buildings which were called in 1441 'the Council House'.

The charter officers of the town were members of the Trinity Gild, while it was the practice for the master of the gild to be chosen from among those who had served as mayor and to sit next the mayor at all public meetings; in 1484 the master of the gild was to take precedence (after the mayor) over the city's officials. Meetings involving smaller numbers took place in the Old Council Chamber, while the treasure of both gild and borough and their 'dedes, muniments, skrowes (rolls), charters' were housed in various chests in 'the Midull Tour chamber', later known as the Treasury – the vaulted chamber on the first floor of Caesar's Tower which can be entered only from the Old Council Chamber. For the town's chest (no longer surviving), the five keys were held, one each, by the mayor, the master of the Trinity Gild, the master of the Corpus Christi Gild, the chamberlains and the wardens. Moreover, the Chair of State is said to have been a double chair for the mayor and the master of the Trinity Gild to sit side by side, and indeed the chair bears the symbols of both borough and gild, the elephant and castle of the city arms and a representation of the Virgin and Child.

After the dissolution of the gilds and chantries, the city acquired St Mary's Hall in 1552 along with other gild properties, and continued to use the Great Hall and the Council House and their auxiliary buildings for the administration of its affairs, for the reception of royal and noble visitors and for other public occasions.

age from the register of Trinity Guild

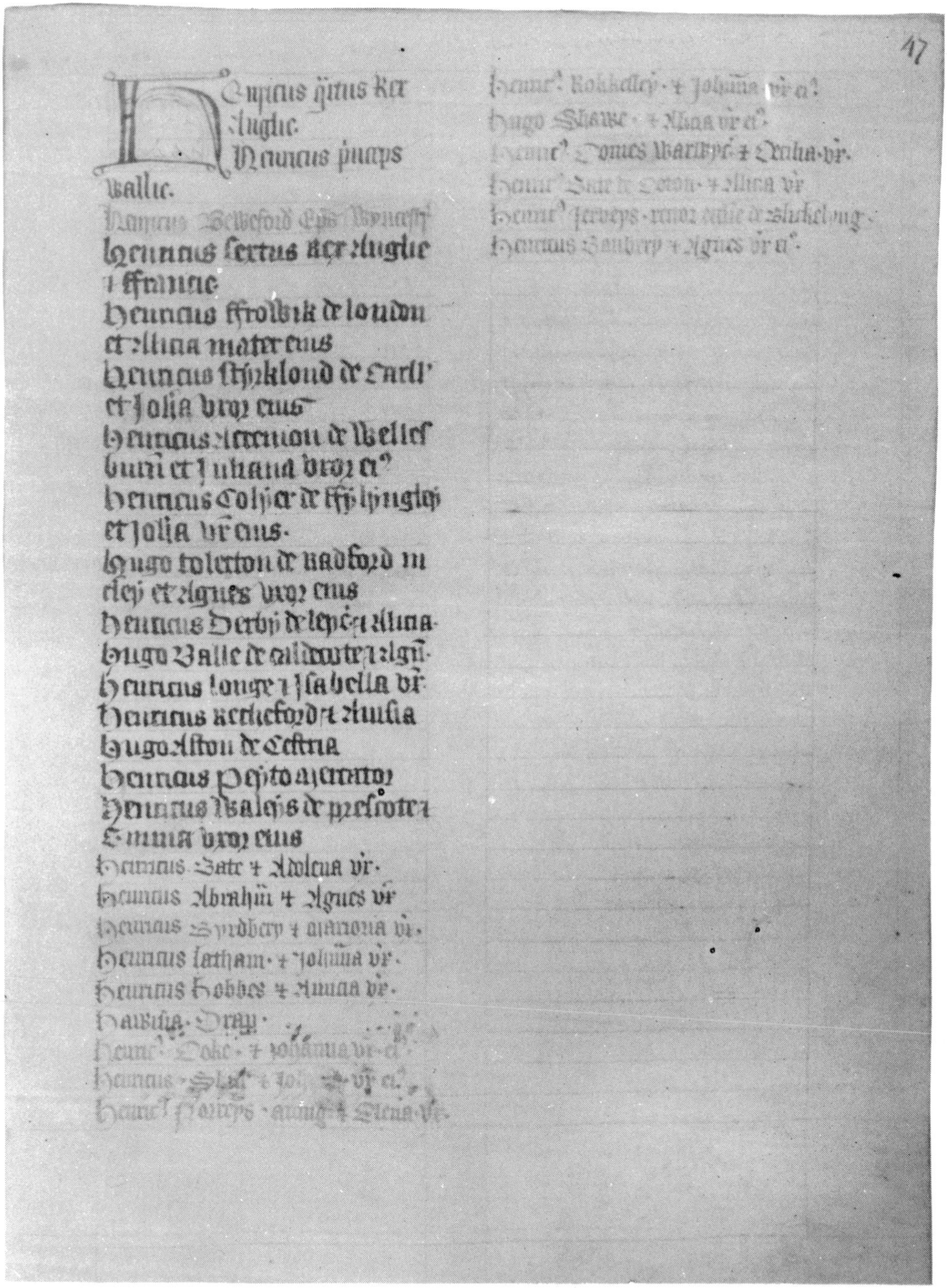

47

Henricus quintus Rex Anglie.
Henricus princeps Wallie.
Henricus Bewford Eps Wynton
Henricus sextus Rex Anglie et Francie
Henricus Frowik de london et Alina mater eius
Henricus Shirklond de Carll' et Johanna uxor eius
Henricus [illegible] de Welles burn et Juliana uxor eius
Henricus Colier de Fyshynglee et Johanna uxor eius.
Hugo Tolerton de Radford in clere et Agnes uxor eius
Henricus Derby de lepe et Alina.
Hugo Balle de Caldecote et Agnes.
Henricus longe et Isabella uxor
Henricus Retheford et Amisia
Hugo Aston de Cestria
Henricus Peyto Armiger
Henricus Walsh de Prestcote et Emma uxor eius
Henricus Bate et Adelena uxor.
Henricus Abraham et Agnes uxor
Henricus Syndbery et Marriona uxor.
Henricus latham et Johanna uxor.
Henricus Hobbes et Anna uxor.
Hawisia Dray.
Henricus Doke et Johanna uxor eius
Henricus Sla[illegible] et Jo[illegible] uxor eius
Henricus [illegible] armiger et [illegible] uxor.

Henricus Rokkelley et Johanna uxor eius
Hugo Shawe et Alina uxor eius.
Henricus Domes Waryke et [illegible] uxor.
Henricus Bate de [illegible] et Alina uxor
Henricus Jerveys [illegible] de [illegible]
Henricus Sanbery et Agnes uxor eius.

The building of St Mary's Hall

See pull out plans at the back

The site on which St Mary's Hall was built in 1340-42 occupied part of the area of the Norman castle of the earls of Chester. It included a stretch of the castle ditch (which followed the line of Bayley Lane) and Caesar's Tower, and at its western boundary adjoined the castle bakehouse. This plot of land (which became part of two tenements fronting on to Earl Street and extending in the thirteenth century to the castle ditch) was granted, towards the end of the century, by Guy de Tyllebroke, vicar of St Michael's church, to William Cole of Coventry and his heirs, who undertook to pay for a lamp to be kept burning before the high altar in St Michael's. While it is known that the gild merchant, in taking over the site, arranged for this responsibility to be discharged annually, it is difficult to establish with certainty the extent of the first buildings there (1340-42) and the precise details of their enlargement (1394-1414), for the surviving gild records comprise only the Gild Register of *c* 1340-1450, an inventory of 1441, some later rentals, and Thomas Sharp's notes and transcripts. From these and other city documents and from the building itself one can however reach tentative conclusions.

On its creation in 1340, the gild made an early start in providing a building in which its members could meet, for its ordinance of 21 September 1342 decreed that the gild's annual meeting was to be held on the feast of the Assumption 'en la salle nostre dame' (in the hall of our Lady). It was probably not an entirely new building, for some of the structures of the by then derelict castle would have been used, partly as foundations, partly as materials for the new edifice. The evidence suggests that part of the south wall of the Kitchen was closely connected with a building of the castle period and that Caesar's Tower (with its north wall perhaps originally extending further westwards) either incorporated the foundations of an earlier building or was perhaps a restored relic of the castle. A deed of 1392 (just before the enlargement) expressly mentions the hall, the tower, three shops (probably facing on to Bayley Lane and built over the filled-in castle ditch) and an entrance gate (crossing the ditch) with a room above it.

The early-fourteenth-century timber-framed structure at the south end of the hall (later known as 'the Council House'), encroaching as it does into the upper part of the Kitchen and having access on both floors to Caesar's Tower, must have been planned all of a piece. Assuming that the two lower rooms of this structure (the Old Council Chamber and the Prince's Chamber) were built in the traditional position as a buttery and pantry, the first Great Hall would have occupied a similar position to that of the present one. This link with the timber-framed Council House, together with the fact that the south wall of the present Great Hall is timber-framed in its upper half, suggests that the first Great Hall may itself have been almost entirely timber-framed. The 1340-42

Gatehouse overlaps the late-fifteenth-century north wall of the present Great Hall, indicating that the Gatehouse had been built as a separate entity and that it was only with the enlargement of 1394-1414 that the old and the new stone buildings were joined to provide a continuous frontage to Bayley Lane. Indeed, in 1411 both rooms in the Gatehouse were still in private occupation and had been over a longish period.

The existence of the three shops mentioned above suggests also that the first Great Hall may not have extended right to Bayley Lane. The Undercroft is divided by a two-foot wall into two chambers. The smaller north one (at a higher level than the main chamber, of slightly different construction – eg, there are no pillars in the responds, there is a lion corbel on the south wall, and white stone has been used in the south wall and in the vaulting – and measuring thirteen feet plus a north wall of four feet) would appear to have been built after the main chamber, which could date from 1340 or even from the thirteenth century. This seventeen-foot later extension covers an area which would have provided space for a row of three shops and is remarkably close to the width of the Red Ditch (probably the southern ditch of the castle) already established by excavation in two of its sections. The external buttresses, correctly placed to take the weight of the walls between the windows of the present Great Hall and evidently added when it was built, do not correspond with the bays of the Undercroft.

Have we then a quickly-run-up timber-framed first Great Hall, built over the main stone Undercroft (a quite normal method of building at this period and especially in Coventry), thirteen or so feet shorter from the north than the interior of the present Great Hall? If this hypothesis is correct, then we have a perfectly good reason for the need both to rebuild and to enlarge the Great Hall (when the northern Undercroft would also have been added) at the end of the fourteenth century when the gilds were amalgamated and the borough was making greater use of it, for the much longer time it took to build, and for the ingenious and unusual juxtaposition of stone and half-timber work we now see.

Tradition says that the stonemasons and woodcarvers working on St Michael's church transferred their labours in 1394 to enlarging and beautifying St Mary's Hall and completed them by 1414. This work then was mainly devoted, if our conclusions are correct, to the construction of a new and longer stone-built Great Hall, which probably included the graceful Oriel (with its carved oak roof and stained-glass windows of birds and roundels of the seasons), framed by a lofty perpendicular arch which screens the entrance to a passage built in the thickness of the buttress. The passage led, on the left, to the half-timbered buttery west of the hall, which may have been taken over or built when the rooms at the south end were occupied for borough business. Sharp, writing in 1824, speaks of its 'richly carved gable' and regards it as 'a very ancient specimen of domestic architecture'. Straight on, the passage led to a doorway (now blocked) and a former balcony, facing on to Bayley Lane, from which proclamations were made. The fine panelled timber roof of the Great Hall, with heraldic bosses at the intersections of the moulded ribs, and angel musicians at the apex of each tie-beam truss, described as sophisticated for its period, must date from the first period of enlargement, since some of the heraldic bosses reflect the reign of Richard II (1377-99). The present roof was then in position by 1400. East and west were six large perpendicular windows and, north of the Oriel, a seventh (high above the passage) which was blocked after 1719. All these and a similar north window may have been glazed by John Thornton of Coventry, the designer of the great east window of York Minster, or by his son.

Almost all trace of the earlier north window however disappeared when the whole wall was reconstructed towards the end of the fifteenth century to take the north window we now see and the notable tapestry below it. These alterations may have been made for the meeting of Henry VII's council in Coventry in 1487 or (more likely) in honour of the occasion when he and his Queen, Elizabeth, were made brother and sister of the Trinity Gild in 1500. The style of both window and tapestry (see pp41-43) suggests the later date. Repairs had been carried out about twenty years earlier to the roof, windows and floor of the hall as well as to the now-vanished battlements of the hall and Caesar's Tower, and the Courtyard was newly paved in 1474. Later alterations and renewals make it difficult to date the timber-framed buildings east and south of the Courtyard, but the medieval staircase to the Great Hall and the fifteenth-century glass later seen in the Drapers' Room (above the Cloister) presuppose the completion of the four sides of the Courtyard along with the enlargement of the Great Hall.

We can say then that, by 1500, St Mary's Hall (in spite of all too fundamental later restorations) had become essentially the complex of buildings we see today.

From the Inventory of the gild's possessions in 1441, we know something of the furnishings of the hall. The present Tournai tapestry was preceded by a cloth of Arras depicting falconry. There seems to have been little furniture except benches, the extra benches and tables for banquets being stored in the Undercroft when not in use. The benches were covered with cloth or tapestry and softened with cushions. The Inventory mentions thirty cushions worked in red and green with elephants or embroidered with heraldic devices, the colours and symbols being those of the city arms.

In the Council Chamber was a table covered with a green cloth, which was marked out in squares (as for an abacus or accounting system), two benches with coverings of red and green, the registers of the gild, a pewter inkstand, a notice concerning payments towards the upkeep of the lamp in St Michael's, a book for the signatures of new members as they took the oath, and two calendars. In the Treasury was a pyx (box) containing the common seal of the city, waxes and keys, the Flemish coffer containing the gild treasure, an iron-bound chest containing the city muniments, two chests of linen and four other smaller chests for various uses. There were standing cups and ewers, chalices and basins of silver and silver-gilt, a cut-glass cup, candlesticks and a cross, mazers (wooden drinking bowls), silver spoons and four table knives. The Kitchen, too, was well supplied with cooking utensils, pans both large and small, spits, racks, pewter vessels and dishes, pots, basins and ewers, cauldrons and coffers.

The Building of St Mary's Hall

Restorations and alterations

See pull out plans at the back

After 1552, when St Mary's Hall became the property of the Corporation and fuller records have survived, continuing expenditure on repairs and renewals can be documented: repairs to masonry, new timber for floors, glazing windows, re-leading roofs, re-paving the Courtyard, painting the outer gates, renewing keys and bolts, mending furniture, cushions and curtains, renewing mats for the Council House, repairing the tapestry, sweeping chimneys, cleaning the hall and the parlours, putting up racks in the Kitchen and replacing Kitchen utensils. At certain times throughout the history of the hall, however, extensive alterations and repairs were carried out, either because of damage, decay or neglect, or in preparation for a royal visit or a banquet.

One such occasion was the visit of the earl of Leicester in 1581. Stonework (including the Mayoress's Parlour, which was perhaps only recently out of private occupation) was whitened, corbels and bosses were painted, the Kitchen was painted, and the pastry ovens, the Gatehouse and the Armoury repaired. The colours used – blue, gold, silver, 'vermysse', verdigris (green), ochre, mastic (pale yellow), vermilion and russet – give some idea of the brilliance of the scene. The services of Durrant (or Durram, who seems to have been the local sign-writer and general painter and copyist) were obtained to inscribe on oak panelling on the east and west walls of the Great Hall verses in Latin and English composed by Philemon Holland who at that time was practising as a physician in Coventry, later became usher of the Free Grammar School and finally its headmaster, but is better known as an eminent translator. Although Holland did not receive payment until 1582, the presence of the earl of Leicester amongst the worthies commemorated (Leofric and Godiva, the Black Prince, kings, queens and nobles) suggests that the inscriptions with heraldic and other devices were completed for the visit. (All the verses are printed, with translations, in Poole's *Coventry* pp 123-25, and two of the Latin ones survive in their original positions, but as replaced in 1826, either side of the dais – see p 46). A tall screen, erected at the south end of the hall to hide the entries to the council rooms and the kitchen stairs, had apparently at its centre a stone structure to which was affixed the brass (now to the right of the door into the Mayoress's Parlour) which commemorates three documents relating to Cheylesmore manor and park, the latest being dated 1568. In front was placed the Chair of State.

A fire in the Council House in 1614 called for considerable expenditure in repairing the damage. Rubble was cleared away and new timber, a new ceiling and tiles (presumably for the roof of the Armoury) were supplied. The next great occasion demanding extensive preparations was the visit of James I in 1617, when stonework was again whitened, the Armoury cleared of its accumulation of rubbish, new glass supplied and the Courtyard re-paved. A payment of 8*d* in

1627 'for laying even the Hall floore after the Salt peeter man had digged there' is explained by the fact that the action of grease and other substances on the earth below a tiled floor formed saltpetre, an ingredient of gunpowder and a Crown monopoly from Tudor times. During the Civil War, when the Armoury, Caesar's Tower and the Undercroft were converted for storing arms and ammunition in large quantities, a new staircase was made from the Great Hall into the Armoury and the floor of the latter was strengthened. At the Restoration, St Mary's Hall was reinstated, the whole place being whitened inside and out, and the arms of Charles I and Charles II, which had been defaced in 1650, being repainted. From then on a yearly 'spring-clean' preceded the All Saints' Day feast. In 1697, Caesar's Tower was repaired and the 'Court' with its seats, table and bar was replaced by a new one. It is not clear where this court was, but perhaps the Mayoress's Parlour had been thus used from earlier in the century.

The eighteenth century saw radical alterations. In the Great Hall, the ancient heraldic tiles (some of which can now be seen in the Oriel and in the Treasury) were replaced in 1755 by wooden boards which raised the floor level to that of the dais, a change which would have marred the fine proportions of the hall. Thirty years later the character of the Mayoress's Parlour was completely altered when the two north windows giving on to Bayley Lane were blocked, the three pointed windows on the Courtyard side were replaced by a Venetian window to improve the lighting from the south, and the walls and ceiling were plastered in contemporary style. (A portion of the cornice and frieze, still to be seen in a cupboard to the left of the present doorway into the Mayoress's Parlour, proves that the room then adjoined the Great Hall and, given its earlier private occupation, suggests that there was originally no open arch on this side to match the arch to the Oriel, but note the similar corbels above the two arches.) The windows on the west side of the Great Hall, destroyed in 1780 during the election riots known as the 'bludgeon fight', were later replaced with plain glass, while the repairs to the north window in 1793 would appear to have done more harm than good.

The most fundamental restoration since the middle ages took place however in 1826 under the direction of Stedman Whitwell when, with the best motives, the restorers stripped the Great Hall and its ancillary buildings of what were regarded as inappropriate additions, replacing early glass and wood carving which was deemed to be either in poor taste or unfit for repair. Unfortunately, the early-fifteenth-century glass remaining in the east windows of the Great Hall was removed and both east and west windows were re-glazed with copies of the medieval glass made to the designs of a Mr Finley by Charles Pemberton of Birmingham, two only of the original figures being retained. Some of the compartments then filled in with plaster were opened up thirty years later and glazed with green diamond-shaped quarries. (The beauty of the original glass is apparent in the two figures retained, which are now in the Old Council Chamber, and in the fragments in the Oriel.) Pemberton may also have added to the confusion in the north window. Philemon Holland's verses on their oak panelling were removed, and the stonework was roughened to take a thick coat of Roman cement on which imitation black-letter copies of the verses and new murals were painted. The Oriel, apparently in a sad state of disrepair, was rebuilt and dimmed or ground glass was inserted, with ribbon-like scrolls containing the names in black-letter of the principal benefactors of the city, those of Leofric and Godiva being distinguished 'by a rich grotesque border in deep yellow'. Some tiles from the original hall floor were laid there and the original oak ceiling was replaced. The arch opposite the Oriel was opened up to form a kind of lobby (to the Mayoress's Parlour) in which the Cheylesmore brass could be displayed, while the screen from which it had been removed was replaced by 'dwarf' screens. The timber-framed buttery (to the west of the hall) was taken down and the two doors from the Oriel passage were blocked.

The Old Council Chamber, said also to be in a 'state of dilapidation and neglect', was restored, in particular the stained glass and the carved gilt entablature. The Elizabethan 'painted cloth' was replaced by coats of arms and other heraldic devices representing the city, the kingdom and benefactors.

George Eld (mayor in 1834-35) re-designed the Mayoress's Parlour, replacing the Venetian window with another of perpendicular style and installing a square-panelled ceiling, stone fireplace, and doors with carved panels, as we see them today. Twenty years later, the two small windows on the north side were re-opened and glazed. The room was used as a police office until 1863 and re-furnished for Council meetings two years later at a cost of £154. A new staircase for access from the ground-floor Cloister and a new entrance across the landing to the Drapers' Room had been constructed with the new offices in 1863.

The Prince's Chamber, formerly the Second Council's meeting place, was fitted up before 1870 as a committee room. In addition, the statue of St George and the Dragon, which was later moved to the Old Council Chamber and is now in the Treasury, was placed over the chimney-piece: two portraits, one of John Neale of Allesley Park, the city's member of parliament on and off from 1722 until 1741 (see p 71) and the other of the Reverend G Greenway, master of the Free Grammar School in 1701, and a copy of Magna Carta completed the decorations. The Old Council

Chamber was again redecorated and cases were installed, first in the Treasury and then in the Council room, for the storage and display of the city's records, until the new 'Gothic' Muniment Room was built for them in 1894. The 1880s saw a further restoration of the Great Hall, when the plaster – and therefore also Philemon Holland's verses – was removed from the walls, and the floor of 1755 was replaced by oak blocks at a lower level. In 1893 the north window was again restored.

During the 1920s and 1930s, the then City Engineer, EH Ford, carried out a large and imaginative programme of restoration. The timber-framed south wall of the Great Hall (plastered over in 1889) and the south window were opened up, the Armoury was reinstated, and the blocked stairway (which had formerly led to a fourth storey – added in 1731 – in Caesar's Tower and which WG Fretton had known about in 1891) was re-discovered (1925). His greatest achievement, however, was the reconstitution of the Old Council Chamber (1936) which was again in a state of decay. It was completely stripped and re-decorated (much as we see it today) to accord with the watercolour of it in the Aylesford Collection, and the two figures from the original east windows of the Great Hall were inserted in the enlarged windows. These had been removed from the Great Hall in 1930 when William Coker Iliffe paid for the re-glazing of the east and west windows to replace the copies of 1826. Finally, in 1938, the two Merton Abbey tapestries, incorporating two of Philemon Holland's Latin verses (now in the body of the Hall), were placed either side of the fifteenth-century tapestry at the northern end of the Great Hall.

The war of 1939-45 presented its own problems: stained glass, tapestry, carved wooden bosses, pictures and furniture were stored for safety. Although St Mary's Hall miraculously survived the concentrated air-raids of November 1940 and April 1941, Caesar's Tower was destroyed by a high-explosive bomb, which also severely damaged the Armoury, shook the fabric of the Council Chamber and the Prince's Chamber and broke up the treasure chest, while fire scarred the roof of the Great Hall. After the end of hostilities, EH Ford undertook, with the help of a team of experienced craftsmen, the restoration of the hall. The roof presented a special challenge. While traditional materials were scarce, a core of steel trusses was used with oak panelling, moulding and tracery (treated against death-watch beetle and dry-rot) to replace charred timbers. Two devoted woodcarvers repaired the carved angels and heraldic bosses, replacing the latter where necessary, and Coventry Art School students painted them in watercolour, before they were restored to the roof. Mr Reg Trotter designed the copper roof which, while slates were unsuitable and lead unobtainable, seemed a reasonable compromise, its attractive green patina being visible from the top of St Michael's tower. With the aid of

Restorations and Alterations

photographs, one of the few remaining skilled stonemasons rebuilt Caesar's Tower with its three storeys and blocked stairway, and the treasure chest was carefully reconstructed. The north window glass, the fragments in the Oriel and the Tapestry were restored to their positions, and the modern glass from the east and west windows was replaced under the supervision of the designer.

Between 1946 and 1948, the Muniment Room was brought up to date with steel shelving for storing the archives, fluorescent lighting and thermostatically controlled heating. The City Archivist's office (originally in the 1863 building) is now temporarily in Broadgate House (with proper facilities for conservation) until more appropriate permanent accommodation can be provided. Storage space in the Muniment Room has long since proved too small and documents are now also stored in the new Council buildings. Finally, in 1954, a floor was inserted in the upper part of the Kitchen (the Kitchen itself being lined with formica and otherwise modernised) and a new bridge constructed to provide access from the Mayor's Parlour (from 1957 the Lord Mayor's Parlour) to the Armoury, which was fitted up for small civic functions.

A general face-lift for the whole complex of buildings is planned (when economic conditions allow) and efforts are being made to find other accommodation for activities which, while in themselves essential, should not be carried on in so rare a building which, now well on into its seventh century of existence, requires protection from the hazards of everyday use.

The Muniment Room

Heat, light, water etc

The original method of heating the Great Hall has not been established, unless a possible louvre formerly in the centre of the roof just south of the dais provided a smoke exit for a central open fire. A heating system, installed in 1857, was renewed in 1890 when the boiler was placed in the westernmost part of the Kitchen below the Prince's Chamber, a position which WG Fretton, writing in 1891, rightly regarded as unsafe.

The lighting, originally by candles, was improved in 1851 when Skidmores installed gas fittings, and in 1899 when electricity was introduced.

Two wells, found in 1856 when rubbish was cleared from the Undercroft, provided the main water supply until 1633, when a lead pipe was installed to bring spring water into the larder and the Kitchen from the city's new piped-water system flowing from an elevated tank on the cathedral site at Hill Top. The pump was later used until, in 1848, a year after the pumping station at Spon End was opened, water was laid on from the mains.

The roofs over the Drapers' Room and the Ante Room still retain leads cast about three hundred years ago, one in 1655 and another in 1690 (both by Thomas Bewley, plumber) and a third in 1726 when Ann Bewley is recorded as the plumber.

In 1710, the mayor and corporation, having been found guilty of embezzling charity funds, were forced to sell their silver plate and, when this was insufficient, the Commissioners sequestrated St Mary's Hall and its contents for six years. One hundred years later, in 1806, the city sold all its pewter, replacing it with delph (crockery) bearing the city's arms.

We have already seen (pp 1-2) something of the interplay between borough and gild and of their respective use of St Mary's Hall. Not only were meetings of the governing body held there and judicial cases heard, but apprentices were sworn in by the mayor, freemen were admitted, bonds were sealed, leases granted, accounts audited, officials sworn in and royal and noble visitors entertained. The Leet dinner took place there, a feast at All Hallows (1 November) and other festivities, and to this day the mayor-making, conferments of the Honorary Freedom, civic luncheons and dinners, town's meetings and other public meetings and receptions are held there.

Trinity Gild feasts were occasions of great splendour. What remain of the accounts of 1533 suggest how frequently and on what occasions the gild found excuse for eating and drinking. On New Year's Day, for instance, the gild clerks, and the priests and clerks of Bablake were granted 6*s*8*d* and 10*s* respectively for a collation; obits in memory of past members involved expenditure for ale, wine, cakes and cheese; a grand feast was laid on for the officers after 'walking the lands' (surveying them and noting dilapidations): there was 'Malvsey', ale and claret, costing 1*s*7*d*, beef, geese, a roast capon, two roast hens and a lamb at 5*s*11*d*, flour, cream and eggs for three custards and a pound of sugar at 1*s*6*d*, cloves, mace, currants, dates, prunes and oranges at 1*s*2*d*, the whole feast costing 12*s*9d; St Matthew's Day, Mid Lent Sunday (our Mothering Sunday), Trinity Sunday, Harvest and Michaelmas were celebrated by eating and drinking; while the receipt of fines and special rents and the entering and auditing of accounts called for refreshments.

Queen Isabella, during her residence at Cheylesmore, probably saw the first St Mary's Hall rise, and the Black Prince, on a visit to Cheylesmore, may well have been there, but for King Henry VI and Queen Margaret, Prince Edward in 1478 at the age of seven, and King Henry VII and his Queen, Elizabeth, was reserved the honour of being admitted in St Mary's Hall as brothers and sisters of the Trinity Gild. Mary Queen of Scots came, not as an honoured guest, but as a prisoner, hurriedly conveyed from Tutbury. By Queen Elizabeth I's command she was delivered over to the mayor for safe-keeping, extra guards were set at the city gates and she was held prisoner in Caesar's Tower. One tradition claims that she was detained in the Mayoress's Parlour, another that she was confined in the castle, which John Stow (writing some ten years later) described as a 'fortelet or pile standing in the earles streite'. This, while strengthening the argument that Caesar's Tower was a relic of the former castle, also supports the view that this was her prison chamber.

We have already seen (p 8) how much work preceded the earl of Leicester's visit in 1581, when he was entertained with a sumptuous feast, every item, including a sum for

The Grille between the Kitchen and the Undercroft from the Undercroft side

flowers, being recorded. Perhaps the most human story is of the little Princess Elizabeth (later Queen of Bohemia) being brought into Coventry from Coombe Abbey at the age of eight. In the telling words of the City Annals, 'the sermon being ended she went to St Mary Hall, where was a Chaire of State sett at the upper End of the Hall. Dinner being ended the Mayor kneeled downe and kissed her Graces hand and gave her a piece of Plate Double Gilt which was three quarters of a yard high, which the Lord Harrington helped her tō receive, because it was too heavie for her to hold, it cost the Citty £29 16*s*8*d*'. Her brother, the young Prince Henry, was entertained in 1611, the year before his untimely death, and there are full accounts of the banquet prepared for their father (James I) in 1617. One could go on quoting expenses for such visits, but one payment of 8*d* to Nicholas Barton and his son for 'watching all nyght in the vault to keep the Cattes from spoyling the cold meates' demands inclusion – clearly food for next day's feast was kept in the Undercroft overnight.

The Civil War brought changes to St Mary's Hall, which became one of Coventry's arsenals. The Armoury was fitted up for storing armour and harness and the Undercroft for ammunition as well as for food. The hall was also used on several occasions to receive Major-General Whaley who commanded the Coventry area.

A few incidental items may serve to illustrate some marginal aspects of the city's history as reflected in the hall. When the people felt in 1388 that the mayor had been too lenient over a case of light-weight bread, they rose and (in St Mary's Hall) 'threw loaves of Bread at the Mayor's head'. A year after the robbery of 1446 the thieves were caught and hanged. The city's ceremonial sword, stolen in 1481, was found four hundred years later on a rubbish heap in London and, after passing through several hands, came to rest in the Burrell Collection in Glasgow.

Cloth was marketed in the hall in the sixteenth century and again in 1727 when the linen, flannel and cloth fairs were held there during the re-building of the Drapers' Hall, and even fish was sold there towards the end of the eighteenth century, while during that and the following century the hall was leased out to all and sundry. About 1860 the Kitchen was used for the dole of soup for unemployed weavers in the slump period, and during the 1939-45 war ration books were stored in the Muniment Room and issued in the Great Hall.

Thus St Mary's Hall, Coventry's mirror for over six centuries, reflecting its economic, social and civic life in its various phases, has been a microcosm of local history and, in so far as they have affected the city, of national affairs also.

Wood Carving of God the Father in the Treasury (P.63).

General Description

An overall view of St Mary's Hall may help the visitor to understand something of the structure of this complex building before embarking on a detailed tour of its several parts. **The northern frontage** to Bayley Lane is continuous from the west wall of the Great Hall *(on your right)* to the Gatehouse and the 1863 building *(on your left)* which extends to St Mary Street. **The west side** of the hall, also continuous, reveals high up a blocked traceried window, with two small passage windows in the buttress below and indications in the masonry of where the Wardens' Buttery once clung to the wall, the Oriel, and the three west windows of the Great Hall, with the windows of the Undercroft below; beyond, the timber-framed gable-end of the Armoury, with the Prince's Chamber below; and (further south) the west side of Caesar's Tower. **The passage** beside the hall, wide enough in 1411 for carts to bring in fuel for the castle bakehouse, evidently pre-dates the hall, and seems to have led also to a garden by the tower. **The south frontage** (seen from the Council House) shows *(to your left)* Caesar's Tower; *(in the centre)* the stone-built Kitchen with the timber-framed Council Chamber and Armoury above; and *(to your right)* the full height of the Kitchen wall, seeming to balance Caesar's Tower, and the end of the 1894 Muniment Room.

See pull out plans at the back

Let us now consider the four blocks of buildings into which the whole complex of St Mary's Hall seems to fall.

1. The Gatehouse, of stone construction and closely linked with the dedication to St Mary, belongs to the first building of 1340-42. It comprises an outer and an inner porch; *to the left (as you enter)* the Mercers' Room; and *above* (straddling both this latter and the two porches) the Mayoress's Parlour, to which there is access both from the Great Hall and through the Courtyard and Cloister.

2. On the east side of the Courtyard *(to the left as you enter from the porch)* is the Cloister just referred to, and range of timber-framed buildings to which it belongs. This probably originated in the early-fifteenth century, but has been much restored and altered. It comprises the Cloister itself (through which there is access on the left to the Mercers' Room and the Mayoress's Parlour, straight ahea the 'new' buildings erected as police and public offices in 1863 to the design of James Murray, and on the right by means of a medieval stair and a Gallery to the Great Hall itself) and *above,* a long room once let out to the Drapers Company.

3. South of the Courtyard *(opposite the Gatehouse)* is a block of buildings of some complexity. With an entry (no admission) from the Courtyard, is the exceptionally interesting Kitchen (not open to the public) on the ground floor. Although (to the Courtyard) this south range is mainly timber-framed, the Kitchen within is stone-built with a massive stone wall on its further or southern side, of which the western portion adjoins Caesar's Tower. Both this latter and masonry in the Kitchen's south wall indicate a Norman origin, with a probable close connection with the earls of Chester's castle which stood on this site. Protruding into the upper part of the Kitchen in its western half is the early-fourteenth-century Council Chamber which, with the Prince's Chamber, and the Armoury above (straddling both rooms and mainly timber-framed), seem to form the building known at least by 1441 as 'the Council House'. At each level – Kitchen, Council Chamber and Armoury – there is an entry to Caesar's Tower. The north face of this timber-framed building (as seen from the Courtyard) has at its first storey the Gallery through which the Great Hall is approached from the main stair, and above it the Ante Room, filling the spac between the Drapers' Room and the south end of the Gre Hall.

4. To the west of the Courtyard is the Great Hall itself, b of stone over a vaulted Undercroft of two chambers (which extends the full length of the Hall) adjoining the Kitchen to the south and having, on its north face to the street, an off-centre doorway with a slightly ogee-shaped lintel, two windows to the left and three to the right. The tracery of th North Window of the Great Hall can best be seen externall and, below it, a blind arcade of nine empty canopied niche providing the interior setting for the Tapestry which hangs beneath this window. *To the right* can be seen the outline the doorway to which the Oriel passage led.

The Armoury and Caesars Tower

DETAILED DESCRIPTION OF ST MARY'S HALL AND ITS CONTENTS

(Arranged according to the recommended itinerary)

ee pull out plans at the
ıck

Ground floor rooms Plan 1
First floor rooms Plan 2
Second floor rooms Plan 3

IH
TH
EP
IH
Anno. Domini. 1590

The Mercers' Room

Plan 1

Part of the Gatehouse of 1340-42, this room has been much altered. In private occupation in 1411 and with its own entrance from the street, it was leased in 1590 for use as their hall to the Mercers' Company who in 1597 blocked this doorway, opening a new one westwards into the porch, which also was later blocked. Yet another door was opened through the south wall of the room, into the Cloister, perhaps in 1710 (see below) and again blocked, while a fourth was cut in the east wall, probably in 1863 or at least when the Magistrates began to use it as a court room. Modern panelling covers these alterations, but the most recent doorway cuts into the **Mercers' Coat of Arms** (quartering the Grocers') for which Durram was paid 11*s*8*d* in 1590. The Mercers first used the room as a second chapel in 1704, relinquishing their chapel in St Michael's nine years later because it was difficult for hearing. Having paid 6*s*8*d* a year for the room, they entered into a new ninety-nine-year lease in 1710 at an annual rent of 40*s* for the chapel, twelve square feet of the Cloister and the use of the Kitchen and the Great Hall for their dinners, but they gave it up in 1789. The room was used as a residence for the Hall Keeper *c* 1843, but by 1870 it had been taken over for corporation business.

It is roughly square and has two square-headed windows on the north side, and one on the south (opening onto the Courtyard), the leading of the clear glass forming the outlines of coats of arms. The **five corbels** on the *north side (west to east)* are: (1) a winged animal; (2) a woman's head with the tongue out; (3) a winged animal with its back leg in its mouth; (4) a bearded head; (5) a winged animal with a human face. The **four corbels** on the *south side (east to west)* are: (1) a contorted winged animal with a jester's face; (2) a bearded head with the mouth open; (3) a crowned green man (that is, with leaves emerging from his mouth); (4) a furry animal head.

Pictures

Thomas Jesson (d 1635) Artist unknown *(south wall)*

A grocer of London and perhaps brother of William Jesson (mayor of Coventry, 1631), Thomas Jesson founded the Jesson charity in Coventry. The portrait, painted in 1636 at a cost of £3, shows Jesson with his left hand resting on a skull, and his coat of arms. The picture was backed with boards in 1638 to 'save it from the wall' and was hung with green sarsenet and ribbon. It was 'refreshed' in 1640 after damage from an overflowing gutter.
(This picture was hanging in the Mayoress's Parlour in 1948)

John Hales (d 1572) Artist unknown *(west wall)*

A Clerk of the Hanaper in the Court of Chancery, John Hales founded the Coventry Free Grammar School, first in the Whitefriars' church and then in St John's Hospital. The date of the portrait is unknown and the inscription *(DD Anna Domina Hales relicta Domini Johannis Hales Baronetti Fundatoris Abnepotis)* refers to its gift by Anne, widow of Sir John Hales of Coventry, descendant of the founder's nephew, to the school in 1704. It probably remained in the old school building until street widening at the end of the century reduced the size of the premises. It is not mentioned again, however, until 1834 when George Eld, then mayor, had it placed in St Mary's Hall, probably in the newly-decorated Mayoress's Parlour, *where it still was in 1948.*

Hales is depicted full-face, three-quarter-length, in a black gown and cap. In his right hand he holds a small book bound in red, and behind his left shoulder is a distant view of the school.

The Porch

Part of the Gatehouse of 1340-42, the **outer Porch** has fifteenth-century **gates.** The outer tierceron star **vault** could be original, but the style of the **bosses** and **corbels**, although some of their subjects are strongly linked with the gild merchant of St Mary, apparently suggests the 1390s. The centre boss of the first vault (as one enters from the street) represents the Coronation of the Virgin; *to the left* is a green man and *to the right* a woman's head. The badly-weathered **corbels** either side of the **second Porch** (as one enters the Courtyard) represent *(to the right)* the Annunciation and *(to the left)* two figures above two animals. The vault is panelled and four-centred. The Porch is broad enough for a carriage entry, but is now approached up two steps.

Detail of Vaulting

Plan 1

The Courtyard

Encapsulating the growth of St Mary's Hall, its beginnings in 1340-42, the re-building of 1394-1414 and the restorations of later centuries, the Courtyard also demonstrates the mixture of half-timber work and old and new masonry. Over the **Porch** is the **Mayoress's Parlour** (part of the 1340-42 stone Gatehouse). *To your left* is a range of much-renewed fifteenth-century timber-framed building, the **Cloister** (once unglazed) *below* with its medieval stair to the Great Hall and entrances to the Mercers' Room and the 1863 building, and *(above)* the **Drapers' Room.** *Opposite you* the ground-floor brick extension conceals the stone-built 1340-42 **Kitchen** which rises, out of sight, to the full height of the other buildings, behind the first-floor timber-framed **Gallery** (also once unglazed) which leads to the Great Hall; and the second-floor jettied **Ante Room.** (The mid-nineteenth-century restoration of the Courtyard was carried out by a Mr Malt, who evidently used some of the materials then discarded for his construction a few years later of Park Cottage when Stoke Park was laid out after 1865.) *To your right* is the east wall of the **Great Hall** of 1394-1414; and below it the **Undercroft**, with two windows (formerly unglazed) and an entry down a flight of steps.

The Porch

The Courtyard

Plan 1

The Undercrofts

There are two Undercrofts. The **main chamber** (now called **the Crypt**), of four bays and about 55 feet long, and two bays and about 28 feet wide, has one entry from the Courtyard and two from the Kitchen (one now blocked), each down a flight of steps; the chamfered vaulting ribs spring, without capitals, from octagonal piers and responds. (**Masons' marks** have been recorded.) The **smaller chamber** at the north end, extending one bay and about 13 feet to Bayley Lane, has an entry down five steps through a four-foot wall from the street and another *(opposite)*, communicating with the main chamber through a two-foot wall and down two steps, a drop of about one foot; the responds lack piers and the southern one has a fine corbel of a leopard or a lion passant. The west wall, five foot nine inches thick, is probably solid, providing a substantial support for the passage above it in the thickness of the buttress. As suggested above (p 5), the main Undercroft may have been built in 1340-42 to support a first timber-framed Great Hall (it could even date from the thirteenth century), the northern Undercroft being added in 1394 to take a lengthened Great Hall re-built in stone.

Both chambers were used for storage, originally perhaps for gild merchandise, frequently for food when a banquet was to take place in the Great Hall above, certainly during the Civil War for ammunition, otherwise for building materials and perhaps more frequently from the eighteenth century as a dumping ground. The '**tavern**', mentioned from time to time from 1469, occupied the northern chamber, which shows evidence of the racking used for storing barrels and had access from the street. Both chambers were cleared in 1856, when two **wells** were found, and were more recently used to store antiquities from other parts of the city. These have been dispersed (some to the Museum), the Crypt now being used for official functions and the smaller north chamber by the Freemen's Guild (incorporated 1946). The latter has five windows to the north and contains the Freemen's guild chair and sideboard and a table to seat twenty-four. On the western wall is a large sculptured stone with interlaced decoration probably of thirteenth-century date.

The **Crypt** has, on its west wall, three square-headed windows, one larger pointed window, and two square **recesses** (probably cupboards); and another recess on the north wall, left of the door. On the east wall are three windows, including a narrow one behind the bar opening into the scullery. The **door** to the Kitchen has original transverse planks and an ancient iron **grille**. The Crypt is embellished with numerous pieces of silver, plaques and coats of arms presented to the city by official visitors, mainly since the 1939-45 war.

The Main Undercroft (The Crypt)

Plan 1

The Cloister or Lower Lobby and Main Staircase

Providing an eastern closure to the Courtyard and a lower storey for the Drapers' Room (above), the much altered and restored fifteenth-century, timber-framed Cloister has given access to the main entrance to the Great Hall at least since the latter's enlargement in 1394-1414, to the Mayoress's Parlour, to the Mercers' Room *c* 1710, to the 'new' buildings from 1863 and to the new Muniment Room from 1894. Glazing, in existence by *c* 1843, was probably introduced in 1826.

The fifteenth-century **staircase**, with its carved oak banisters and ceiling timbers (with pre-Tudor roses) makes a fitting approach to the Great Hall. Of especial interest are the two **carved heads** finishing the lower ends of the banisters, one of a man *(on the left)*, the other of a woman in fifteenth-century head-dress *(on the right)*.

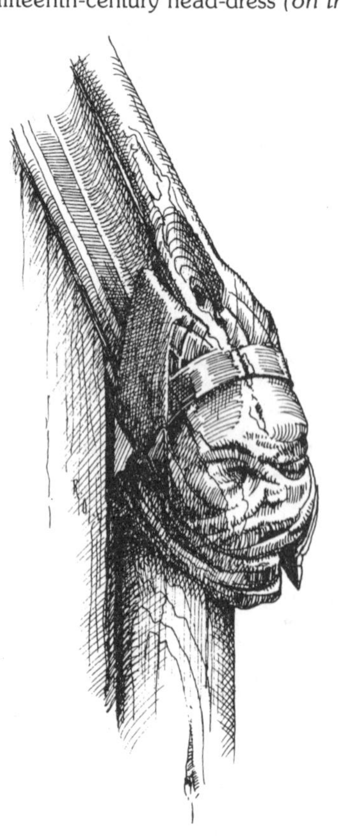

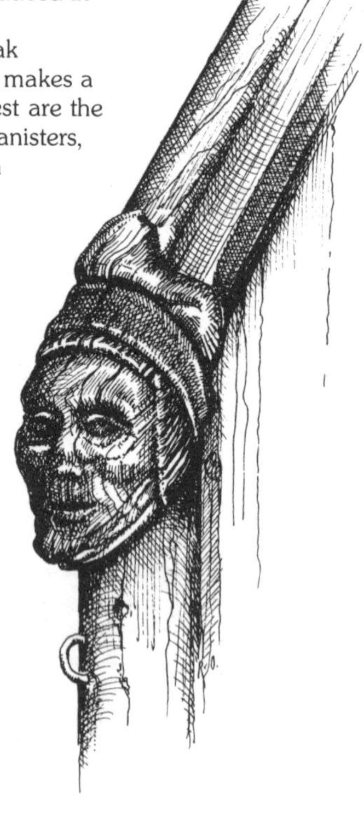

Two carved heads, lower ends of the bannisters

The Gallery or Upper Lobby

This, the ante-room to the Great Hall, is entered from the medieval staircase through a modern door and leads, via a studded door of two leaves, into what was probably originally the screens passage at the south end of the Great Hall. The Gallery was unglazed, probably until 1826. *To your left* are two **tapestries** of classical subjects, with soldiers and senatorial figures, and perhaps set in North Africa, but it is difficult to place the Chinese figure in the third section. While they are undoubtedly a pair (note the bird with three nestlings – or a pelican in her piety – at each of the four top corners, and the similar swags and four columns of flowers and fruit which date the tapestries to the seventeenth or eighteenth centuries), can we discount the tradition that one was found by the Hall keeper stuffed up a chimney? William Reader purchased at least one of them at the Palace Yard sale in 1822, the mayor, George Eld, re-purchasing it from him in 1834 for St Mary's Hall. They were first used as framed screens in the Great Hall and were later installed in their present position.

Plan 2

The Great Hall

(To understand the following descriptions, imagine yourself standing near the south end of the hall and facing towards the north window)

This, to all intents and purposes, is the Great Hall of 1394-1414, roughly 70 feet long, 29 feet wide and 33 feet high, the north, west and east walls and the lower half of the south wall being built of stone. Probably the masonry of the **south wall** *(behind you)*, the timber-framing above it and a wider, slightly lower Minstrels' Gallery were present in the Hall of 1340-42. The **north wall** *(at the further end)* was reconstructed at the end of the fifteenth century to take the new **North Window** and the **Tapestry** below it. The tall archway *on your right* was opened in 1826 opposite the original arch to the **Oriel** *on your left.* The fourteenth-century **roof**, which was damaged by fire during the 1939-45 war, was restored during the succeeding decade. (Note the **plaque** inside the main door *on your right*, and see p 11 .) The North Window has late-fifteenth-century **glass** and the Oriel earlier fragments; the modern glass (1930) in the six perpendicular windows *(east and west sides)* replaces glass installed in 1826.

The Roof

Of panelled construction, with tie-beam trusses and ribs, this splendid example of a late-fourteenth-century timber roof has ten **angel musicians**, two facing each other from each of the trusses which divide the roof into five compartments equivalent to the five bays of the building. Some play the 'crwth' (crowd, played like a fiddle), trumpet, 'cittern' (plucked and somewhat like a guitar), harp and bass flute. At the intersections of the moulded ribs are heraldic **bosses**, fifteen to each compartment, including the white hart of Richard II, a swan, pelican, griffin, unicorn, elephant and castle, green man, horse, crowned lion and jester. (For details of the post-war restoration, see p11 .)

Roof Boss

The Corbels

These stone carvings, just above eye level and finishing off the wall posts which support the roof, are contemporary with the hall and difficult to understand. They seem to represent *(on the left from the south)*: (1) head with badly eroded head-dress; (2) head and shoulders, hands joined, and another hand seeming to descend left of the head (the Trinity?); (3) bearded head, crowned; *above the arch to the Oriel* (off-centre): queen's head and shoulders, hands joined; *opposite, above the arch to the Mayoress's Parlour* (centred): another queen's head and shoulders, one hand to bodice; *(on the same side from the north)*: (1) head with cushion behind and crown above; (2) bearded head, crowned; (3) bearded head with tiara, hand raised in blessing – but there appears to be a monkey to the right – this is possibly the head of St Peter, since the beard is indicated by lines.

The East and West Windows

These graceful windows, with their modern stained glass, originally contained early-fifteenth-century stained glass almost certainly designed by John Thornton of Coventry (designer of the famous east window in York Minster) or by his son. The dates of the subjects (listed below) suggest two or three distinct periods of work, one probably completed by 1404 before John Thornton went to York, the second *c* 1414, and a possible third *c* 1433. The windows have suffered badly over the centuries. Humfrey Wanley (son of the vicar of Holy Trinity church, Coventry, and librarian to Robert and Edward Harley, earls of Oxford), who visited St Mary's Hall in 1719, found them already 'so defaced and broken' that it was diffcult to identify the figures. When election riots in 1780 destroyed the glass in the west windows, plain glass was put in, but the restorers of 1826 scrapped the east windows as well, preserving only two heads from the main lights, which were inserted in the new windows, and in 1930 placed (where you can now see them) in the Old Council Chamber (see p58). There may also be some fragments in the Oriel. The enamel-painted glass of 1826, which was said at the time to be a faithful copy of the originals (see p 9), soon began to fade and was replaced in 1930 by the gift of William Coker Iliffe. On the advice of Bernard Rackham, Mary Dormer Harris and Alderman Grant, who also approved the design, the work was entrusted to Clayton and Bell. The twenty figures listed were to include fourteen of the original subjects:

Stored in the basement of Caesar's Tower for safety during the war, but only slightly damaged, the glass was restored by Reginald Bell and replaced in 1952-53.

est side reading from the south

t window

hn Onley, mayor, 1396 and 1418	
lliam Whitchurch, mayor, 1400	○◇
bert Shipley, mayor, 1402 and 1416	◇
chard Sharp, mayor, 1433 and 1450	◇

d window

omas Arundel, archbishop of Canterbury, 396-1414	□○◇
chard Crosby, prior of Coventry, 398-1437	□○◇
hn Burghill, bishop of Coventry and chfield, 1398-1414	□○◇
oger Walden, bishop of London, 1404-6	□○◇

rd window

illiam Beauchamp, Lord Abergavenny, 1411	□○◇
hanna, his wife, *d* 1435	□○◇

East side reading from the north

1st window

Richard Beauchamp, earl of Warwick, 1403-39	□○◇
Isabell, his wife, *d* 1440, sister of the Trinity Gild	□○◇

2nd window

Queen Isabella, wife of Edward II, *d* 1358	
Edward the Black Prince, *d* 1376	○
Richard II, 1377-99	□
Sir William Babyngton, *d* 1455	□◇■

3rd window

Humphrey, earl of Stafford, 1403-60	□○◇■
John, duke of Bedford, 1414-35	□○■
Humphrey, duke of Gloucester, 1414-47	□○■
John Mowbray, duke of Norfolk, 1425-32, lord of Caludon Castle	□○◇

gures included in Dugdale's MS list of 1653	□
ose included in the 1826 windows	◇
rothers of the Trinity Gild	■
those mentioned by Wanley in 1719. Of the earl of Stafford and the duke of Norfolk he says: 'there are inscriptions above them but out of Reach of my Spectacles'	○

The North Window before the Tapestry was re-hung

The North Window

The tradition claiming John Thornton as the designer of the North Window cannot be substantiated. While he probably designed the first window, the reconstruction of the north wall to take the new window and tapestry at the end of the fifteenth century, took place long after his death. The tracery is late-fifteenth-century in style and the design and workmanship of the glass, akin to those of the king's glaziers of Westminster of the same period, are regarded by Bernard Rackham, writing in 1931, as 'probably one of the best products of the royal workshops in purely English style'. The figures are kings of England (actual or legendary), taken *chronologically*: Constantine, Arthur, William I, Richard I, Henry III, Edward III, Henry IV, Henry V and Henry VI. The coats of arms in the tracery lights are: City of London, *Coventry, *earls of Hereford, earls of Chester, King Ethelred, King Alfred, Edward III, Henry VI, kings of East Anglia, Constantine, duke of Aquitaine, duke of Normandy, earl of Lancaster, earl of Cornwall, *King Alfred's cross, *Leofric, kings of Man, City of York.

The restoration and re-leading of 1793 seem to have resulted in damage and utter confusion in both figures and inscriptions. Thomas J Grylls of Burlison and Grylls carried out the expert rearrangement, restoration and re-leading of 1893, stating in the leaflet issued at the time that, of the coats of arms listed by Dugdale, only fourteen remained. While most of the glass is original, fragments removed from the window at this latest restoration were placed in the Oriel.

**new glass added in 1893*

The Tapestry

A rare and highly decorative Gothic piece, this Tapestry is of outstanding importance because, while in itself it is of great beauty, it is also unique in that it remains virtually complete and in the position for which it was designed at the end of the fifteenth century. It is good quality Tournai work, closely linked by the distinctive textile pattern on the robes of the king, the queen and the Virgin, and other decorative elements, with a group of well-attested Tournai tapestries of *c* 1500 associated with the weaver, Arnould Poissonnier. The three vertical divisions of the Tapestry according with the three divisions of the window above, the presence of Tudor roses in the border and the style of the costumes confirm the view that it was commissioned for its present position below the new North Window and on a newly constructed wall, all in preparation for the visit of King Henry VII and his Queen, Elizabeth, in 1500 for their ceremonial admission to the Trinity Gild.

The Tapestry has six compartments, three above and three below. *In the centre of the lower half* is represented the Assumption of the Virgin; *to the left* Henry VII kneels, accompanied by courtiers, with *(in the compartment above)* apostles and saints, each with an emblem; *to the right* Elizabeth kneels, attended by courtiers, with *(in the compartment above)* female saints; *in the centre compartment above* is the only intrusive element, probably of the Commonwealth period, although the only relevant entries in the records for work on the Tapestry are for repairs in 1519 (26*s*8*d*) and 1583, and a payment of 40*s* in 1604 to Thomas Carpenter for 'trimming the orrys Clothe'. Originally this compartment contained a representation of the Trinity, God the Father indicated by the Hebrew inscription for Jehovah, and the Crucifixion by the Instruments of the Passion. In its place is now a figure of Justice.

Cleaned and restored by the Textile Conservation Centre at Hampton Court Palace, the Tapestry was replaced in St. Mary's Hall in 1981.

The Dais

At either side of the fifteenth-century Tapestry are two of Philemon Holland's **Latin verses** which, with his English verses, had first been inscribed in black-letter on oak panelling round the Great Hall in 1581 (see p 8), but in 1826 were copied onto Roman cement. The verse *on the left* is in honour of former kings and queens, but principally of the reigning sovereign in 1581, Elizabeth I, with her coat of arms, that *on the right* in honour of Edward the Black Prince, with his coat of arms. (A quotation from **Ecclesiasticus** xliv, 8-9, probably inscribed in the same way in 1826 – and badly worn – remains *at the south end of the west wall).* The **two modern tapestries**, woven by the Morris Art Workers, Merton Abbey, in 1938 for the dais, are now in the body of the Hall.

The dais was an original feature of the Great Hall and the proportions of the hall suffered when, in 1755, the original tiled floor was taken up (some of the tiles are now in the Oriel and in the Treasury) and wooden boards brought the level of the main floor up to that of the dais, an error which was corrected in the 1880s when a wood-block floor was installed at a lower level. The **bench** *on the north side* of the dais was said *c* 1843 to be original, and may date from the fifteenth century.

The Oriel

A roundel from the oriel inscribed 'September'

Probably part of the Great Hall of 1394-1414, this graceful bay window framed by a lofty arch is a characteristic feature. In a poor state of repair, it was rebuilt in 1826. Lists of benefactors in black-letter on scrolls, and a 'rich grotesque border in deep yellow' then inserted were later replaced by the fragments of glass we now see there. An **inscription** *in the upper stage* states: 'The fragments of old glass placed in this window were removed from the large North window at the time of its restoration, 1893'. We may doubt that all of it came from the North Window, unless fragments of other glass had been introduced there in 1793, but it probably represents all that remained (apart from the North Window and the figures later inserted in the Old Council Chamber window) of the **original glass** in St Mary's Hall.

It is too fragmentary to attempt a comprehensive description, but close scrutiny reveals several human faces and fragments of human anatomy, angels' wings, parts of inscriptions, pieces of canopies and pinnacles; *in the lower stage*: a complete **roundel** *(second left-hand panel)* showing a man threshing corn and inscribed 'September'; fragments of another **roundel** *(second central panel),* a claw of Leofric's eagle and a piece of chequer-board; another **roundel** *(first right-hand panel)* of cutting the corn; and *(second panel)* a sheep grazing – perhaps part of another roundel – some brilliantly coloured later fragments and a part of a date – 16--; *in the upper stage*: several fragments of heads, including a fine bearded one; a bishop's mitre, a church, a

The Oriel

bright yellow open box and chequered tiled floors *(first centre panel),* a figure, perhaps St Catherine, with an open book *(second centre panel).* Bernard Rackham mentions also the hand of St John the Baptist holding the Agnus Dei and suggests that some of the glass came from the Drapers' Room where Wanley in 1719 had seen fifteenth-century glass including figures of St John the Baptist and St Catherine and an inscription mentioning Henry Peyto (mayor, 1423). We should not discount the possibilty that some of the earlier fragments are from John Thornton's hand, designed for the Oriel itself, for the East or West Windows, or even for the first North Window.

The floor **tiles** are from the Great Hall, and the carved oak roof is a copy (made in 1826) of the original. The **sideboard**, either reconstructed for its present position from an earlier piece of Elizabethan date or installed in 1581, may be the one Wanley saw there in 1719. The **two statues** *high up on either side of the arch* came from the Coventry Cross (put up in 1422, replaced in 1541 and taken down in 1771); both hold books. Also standing in the Oriel is a **statue of Lady Godiva** by WC Marshall, who exhibited a sculpture of Lady Godiva (probably this one) at the Royal Academy in 1854. It appears in a watercolour of the Oriel dated 1878.

To the right of the arch is a **passage,** fourteen feet long and three feet wide, within the thickness of a buttress, which leads towards the north wall. It originally gave access on the left to the timber-framed Wardens' Buttery which until 1826 clung to the west side of the hall (signs of its former presence can still be seen on the outside wall below the blocked window), and straight ahead to a doorway (now blocked but its outline still visible on the north wall) and balcony from which proclamations were made.

A roundel from the oriel 'Cutting the Corn'

R.O. 80

The Portraits

After the middle ages (when stained glass and tapestry had been the media for depicting local and national personages), St Mary's Hall, like other gild and borough halls, began to be adorned with paintings in oils of royalty and local worthies. Sometimes originals by well-known artists, sometimes copies by a local man of lesser talents, they are always of interest. In 1948, St Mary's Hall had a mixture of the good and the ordinary, royal portraits from an alleged Mary Tudor to George IV and a good range of local benefactors. Since then, however, the staff of the Herbert Art Gallery have arranged for the conservation of the best of them and their proper protection in the gallery itself. *(A list of these appears in an Appendix, p* 71 . Portraits of Edward VII, George V, and Edward VIII as Prince of Wales by Joseph Mordecai (*c* 1852-1940), were presented by the artist's widow (1944-45) to be hung in St Mary's Hall pending a place in the Art Gallery. Since St Mary's Hall was as yet unrestored, the portraits were hung instead in the County Hall.)

The following royal portraits remain in the Great Hall: two, *either side of the North Widow,* the one *on the west* of **George IV** (although presented in 1832 by William IV and said *c* 1843 by Sharp to be an original by Sir Thomas Lawrence, this is a studio copy of the original in the National Gallery of Ireland); the one *on the east* of **Queen Caroline**, wife of George II (after Kneller's portrait of 1716 in the Royal Collection); *at the south end* and best seen from the Minstrels' Gallery: *on the west (above)* **James II** (painted in 1683 as duke of York by 'Mr Ellis the Limner'); *(below it)* **George I** (artist unknown), the portrait being presented to the city in 1719 by Sir Adolphus Oughton, member of Parliament for Coventry, 1715-37; *on the east (above)* **William III** (artist unknown), purchased in London in 1691 together with a portrait of Mary II for £10; *(below it)* **Charles II** (painted in 1681 by 'Mr Ellis the Limner') and restored in 1683 by Richard Launder.

Probably, with its fourteenth-century decoration, a feature of the first St Mary's Hall and later raised and narrowed, the Minstrels' Gallery is set against the background *(above it)* of the timber-framed south wall of the Great Hall (plastered over in 1889 and uncovered again *c* 1926), and *(below it)* of masonry (framing the Prince's Chamber, the stairs to the Kitchen and the Old Council Chamber), which also forms the upper part of the north wall of the Kitchen (see p 68). The Gallery, as its name implies, was used by the minstrels and waits who provided music and entertainment on festive occasions.

With the Armoury behind, it is an appropriate setting for the city's collection of **armour**, which can best be seen from the hall. There are thirteen suits, the one in the centre being almost complete and comprising a helm*, collar, corslet (body armour), taces (skirt), vambraces (forearm) and greaves (leg); on either side is a suit of head-piece, corslet and taces; ten Elizabethan suits of head-piece and corslet; and twelve pikes. The city's accounts include numerous entries for the purchase of armour, and a full inventory exists of armour owned by the city in 1589, some pieces being then 'in the gallery'.

The Minstrels' Gallery

(as seen from the north end of the hall)

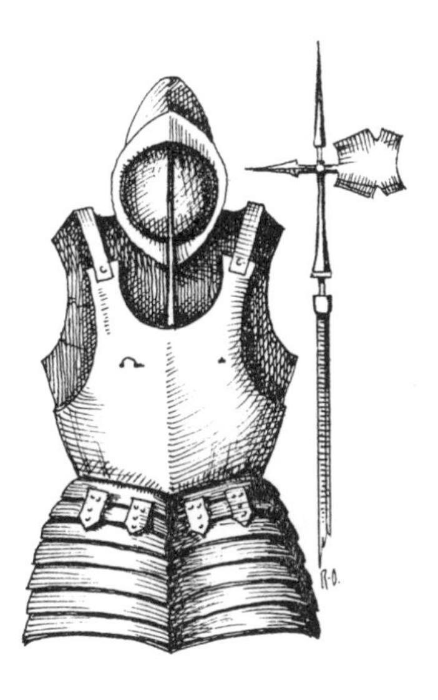

Armour in the Minstrels' Gallery

* *The rare salade or sallet (light helmet) of the period of the Wars of the Roses, which this helm replaces, is now preserved in the Museum.*

The Minstrels' Gallery

Above the Gallery is a new **window,** introduced in 1926 as the gift of Alderman Malcolm Kenneth Pridmore, the glass to the design of Reginald Bell. The subject is Leofric and Godiva, with the inscription below: 'She took the tax away and built herself an everlasting name – Tennyson'. The words 'Camera Principis' (the Prince's Chamber – referring to the Black Prince) are repeated diagonally across the window. It is possible that a piece of wooden tracery, formerly in the main Undercroft, had been removed when this new window was installed. (In 1855 a large picture, 'Bacchus and Ariadne' by Luca Giordano (1632-1707), was presented by Edward Ellice, member of parliament for the city, with the specific intention of helping to form an art gallery, and was hung above the Minstrels' Gallery. Now in the Herbert Art Gallery, it is in the course of restoration.

The South Window

She took the Tax away
and built herself an
everlasting name.
R.O. 85

The Mayoress's Parlour

Part of the 1340-42 Gatehouse and probably in private occupation during the fourteenth and fifteenth centuries, this room may not have been accessible from the Great Hall until *c* 1580 and may then have been used as a court room, but by 1719 it was known as the Mayoress's Parlour and was being used for the mayoress and 'the better sort of Women' to dine apart at public feasts. Access from the Great Hall is now through a lofty arch, similar to the one opposite framing the Oriel, and up six steps. This arch was not opened until 1826, when the small doorway, which previously led directly into the room, was replaced to provide a grander, lobbied entrance. Note *(to the right of the door)* the **brass** commemorating the duke of Northumberland's grant of Cheylesmore manor and park to the city in 1549, its confirmation by Elizabeth I, and the city's undertaking of 1568 to observe the regulations laid down. The brass was moved to its present position in 1826 when the screen at the south end of the Great Hall, on which it had been fixed in 1581, was taken down. The remains of a piece of **cornice and frieze** (which can still be seen *in the cupboard on the left within the arch)* not only shows what the new decoration was like when the room was stripped and plastered in 1785, but also indicates that the Parlour then extended right up to the east wall of the Great Hall.

Meanwhile, the alterations of 1826 must have left the Parlour in a poor state and in 1834-35 the then mayor, George Eld, undertook its restoration virtually to the form in which we see it today. The Venetian window of 1785 was replaced by a **five-light window** in perpendicular style, the present stained glass being added in 1888; the walls and ceiling were newly plastered and the latter ornamented with carved wooden mouldings and bosses; the stone **fireplace** is in Tudor style, the tracery on the jambs being copied from that in the banqueting hall at Kenilworth Castle; the carved **doors** also date from this period. The two north windows, blocked in 1785, were re-opened and glazed in 1854. After 1863, the Parlour was fitted up for meetings of the Council, and new furniture (mainly copies of earlier furniture) was made at a cost of £154.

Above the fireplace is the very simple, very moving **equestrian statue of Lady Godiva** by William Behnes (1795-1864) who, trained as a pianoforte manufacturer, became a student at the Royal Academy in 1819, his reputation for portrait busts being high between 1820 and 1840.

EXIT

Plan 2

The Drapers' Room

Scratchings from the window in the Draper's Room

Situated above the Cloister and approached from the Mayoress's Parlour or by the staircase in the 1863 building, this room dates from the fifteenth century. (Note the early-fifteenth-century **carving** filling the spaces between tie-beams and rafters.) The ten square-headed latticed windows, with coats of arms formed by the leading, contained fifteenth-century glass when Wanley saw them in 1719. *Over the door from the landing* is a **bust of Sir Joseph Paxton** (1801-65), member of parliament for Coventry from 1854 until his death, designer of the Great Exhibition buildings of 1851, and also of the Coventry London Road cemetery; and *on the walls of the landing* are seven large **canvas tables recording the names of the mayors of Coventry** from 1348 – the first mayor (John Ward) is now known to have been chosen in 1346. (They were on the landing of the old staircase in 1840 and restored to the new staircase in 1864).

From 1430 the town clerk occupied a room in St Mary's Hall for which he paid rent to the Trinity Gild and which may have been this room which was leased to the Drapers' Company at a rent of 3*s*4*d* a year in 1558, when it was described as 'a chamber in seynt marie hall over the steyres'. The Drapers were still occupying the room in 1618, when they had presses and boxes installed and a 'chekker' for accounting, but probably ended their tenancy when their new hall was built in 1727. The floor was lowered in 1863, the south wall plastered and a stairway and small entry to the Ante Room made to replace an earlier communication.

The Prince's Chamber

The traditional name of this room, derived from the Black Prince's association with Coventry, has also been applied to the city itself (it appears on the city's coat of arms as 'Camera Principis') and to St Mary's Hall as a whole. Little however is known about the room which was probably used as the buttery or the pantry from 1340-42 until it was needed for borough affairs. It was certainly used by the Second or Common Council in 1623, although the Clothiers' Company were allowed to use it in 1651 for their quarterly meetings at a rent of 20s a year. By 1870 it had been furnished as a committee room, but in 1901-2 the room was thoroughly restored and the walls lined with **oak panelling** from an old house on the Council House site, the Jacobean **overmantel** coming from the same source. The **refectory table** is a composite piece made from oak removed from houses in High Street in 1928 and presented to the city in 1937 by Evan OC Howells. The **sideboard**, a strange medley of medieval continental work with suggestions of oriental influence has *(on the back)*: two crowned knights in chain armour, a soldier with a quartered shield, and a figure praying, with a feline head below; *(on the lower part)*: an oriental subject against a jungly background. After 1948, the room was used for a time as the City Archivist's office.

Plan 2

The Old Council Chamber

Probably (like the Prince's Chamber) the original buttery or pantry for the first St Mary's Hall of 1340-42, this room (entered through a single studded door with two handles) remained when the new Great Hall was built in 1394-1414. Although the 'Domus Concilii' (Council House) is not referred to until 1441, the mayor's council had probably begun to use it by 1421. It then has a more or less unbroken history as the Council Chamber until the Mayoress's Parlour was fitted up for council meetings soon after 1863.

We know something of its furnishings in 1441 (see p6) and of later items such as new matting and repairs and renewals. In the early-nineteenth century there was a 'throne-like seat' for the mayor, a large table for account books and seats round it 'with stall embelishments' (probably the **dark-oak benches with poppy-heads** still there), hangings bearing the arms of Elizabeth I, an elaborate carved entablature round the walls and a flat panelled ceiling with carvings. The room did not escape the restorations of 1826, when the former hangings of painted cloth were replaced by the city arms over the mayor's raised seat at the north end, the arms of England on one side between the cognizances of the Black Prince and Henry VI, and on the other the arms of the marquis of Hertford and the earl of Craven, the last two city recorders. The city arms and other devices were displayed in stained glass in a small window, with an inscription recording the restoration by James Weare, mayor.

By 1871, the room had been fitted up with glass cases for some of the records; and by 1888, when the Society of Antiquaries' Cocked Hat Club visited St Mary's Hall under WG Fretton's guidance, some of the city's insignia were also on display there. The most recent restoration was in 1936 when EH Ford made every effort to restore the room to as near its original state as possible. The **oak panelling** came from the Coventry Arms (demolished a few years earlier), the oak ceiling and floor were renewed, the **window** was enlarged to take fifteenth-century glass from the Great Hall, G Milton of Coventry restored the carved oak **entablature,** and the Morris Art Workers, Merton Abbey, wove the new **tapestry** to the design of Macdonald Gill. The tapestry design represents *(beginning left of the entry)*: the priory seal, Leofric's eagle, the earls of Chester's three garbs (sheaves), the Black Prince's feathers and a sequence of royal arms – Richard II, Henry VI, Mary, Elizabeth I, Charles II(?) and George V, together with devices such as a white hart, catherine wheel, griffin, eagle and Tudor roses, all representing facets of the city's history.

The fifteenth-century **stained glass** in the south windows is the main surviving portion of the original east windows of

Front view of the Gild Chair

Details of the Virgin and Chi[ld] on the left arm of the Gild Chair

the Great Hall and represents *(in the centre lights)* Thomas Arundel (archbishop of Canterbury, 1396-97 and 1399-1414), and Richard Sharp (mayor of Coventry, 1433 and 1450), and *(to the left)* the arms of Beauchamp, and *(to the right)* the arms of Beauchamp and Fitzalan. An **inscription** records their removal to their present position in 1930. (Bernard Rackham, writing in 1931, seems to suggest that the first figure is that of John Burghill (bishop of Coventry and Lichfield, 1398-1414), while Richard Sharp, the second figure and the latest of the subjects, does not appear in the earliest lists, see p39.)

Of outstanding importance is the intricate and beautiful **Gild Chair** of *c* 1450, originally either a double chair for the mayor and the master of the Trinity Gild to sit side by side, or the mayor's seat attached to a bench perhaps in St Michael's, but this is less likely. As the mortices suggest, it is incomplete, and the figure of the **Virgin and Child** *on the left arm (as you face the chair)* has no complement on the right arm. Surmounting the back are *(on the right),* which would have been the centre of a double chair the **elephant and castle** of the city arms, and *(on the left)* a **crown supported by two lions** – an indication that the chair may date from the reign of Edward IV (1461-83). So far it has not been possible to explain an entry of 1579 in the City Accounts: 'pd for carrage of the chere from St Nicholas Hall to St Mary Hall, vid'. A further entry in 1585 of a payment of 16*d* to the carpenter for making stairs to the chair (two days' work) suggests an entirely new arrangement, and indeed we know that the 'Chair of State' was placed in front of the new screen at the south end of the Great Hall in 1581. It seems to have remained in the Great Hall until it was moved to the Mayoress's Parlour probably when the latter was fitted up for council meetings after 1863.

The **poppy-head bench-ends**, though much cut about and attached to portions of a carved screen, may have come in the first place from the Whitefriars after the dissolution of the monasteries. The oak table (*c* 1605-10, from Charlcote Hall) was purchased in 1903 for £20. Some of the chairs bearing the elephant and castle are of some antiquity, others are likely to be later copies.

The Treasury

Plan 2

Approached from the Old Council Chamber through a single, studded door, a small panelled lobby and the original massive single, studded **Treasury door** of solid oak (with further strengthening inside, three iron bolts moved by separate keys, an ancient strong handle and three chains), the Treasury is on the first floor of Caesar's Tower and was described in 1451 as 'the Midull Tour chamber'. This small, low room has a tierceron star **vault,** a square-headed window at either end and a fine **tiled floor** of both plain and heraldic tiles. The latter include a chequer board, white hart, fleur de lys, eagle and floriated cross, on others lettering. They may have come from the Great Hall when the original floor was replaced.

The **Treasure Chest** would appear, from the iron work, to date from the thirteenth century and therefore pre-dates both gild and borough. It has three locks and massive hinges and may be the 'Flemish coffer' referred to in 1441 (see p 7). Broken up during the 1939-45 war when Caesar's Tower was destroyed, it has been meticulously restored.

The Treasury

Plan 2

The **Wood carvings,** which are known to have been fixed on the Old Council Chamber ceiling since at least c1810, were removed several years ago for cleaning and examination. Of early-fifteenth-century English workmanship, these superb carved oak figures may well have come from a screen or an altar-piece in one of the Coventry churches. They represent: God the Father, the Virgin and Child, St John the Baptist with the Agnus Dei, St Michael fighting the devil, St Catherine and her wheel, an angel (possibly Gabriel) and an eagle (perhaps symbolising the Word of God). The iconography suggests a conscious choice of this particular selection of figures for St Mary's Hall. They are now displayed standing, rather than in their former position, since they were clearly intended to be seen thus.

Wood carving of the Virgin and Child

Wood carving of St. Catherine and her wheel

The wooden statue of **St George** (in armour) **and the Dragon** (*c*1470-90) is firmly modelled, though with the stumpy figure-work which suggests a provincial origin in the late-fifteenth century. It lacks the dynamic treatment of the same theme in an alabaster of fifty years earlier, with which it has been compared, but it is an independent work with its own special appeal. It was brought from St George's Chapel on Gosford Bridge when the chapel was demolished in the nineteenth century.

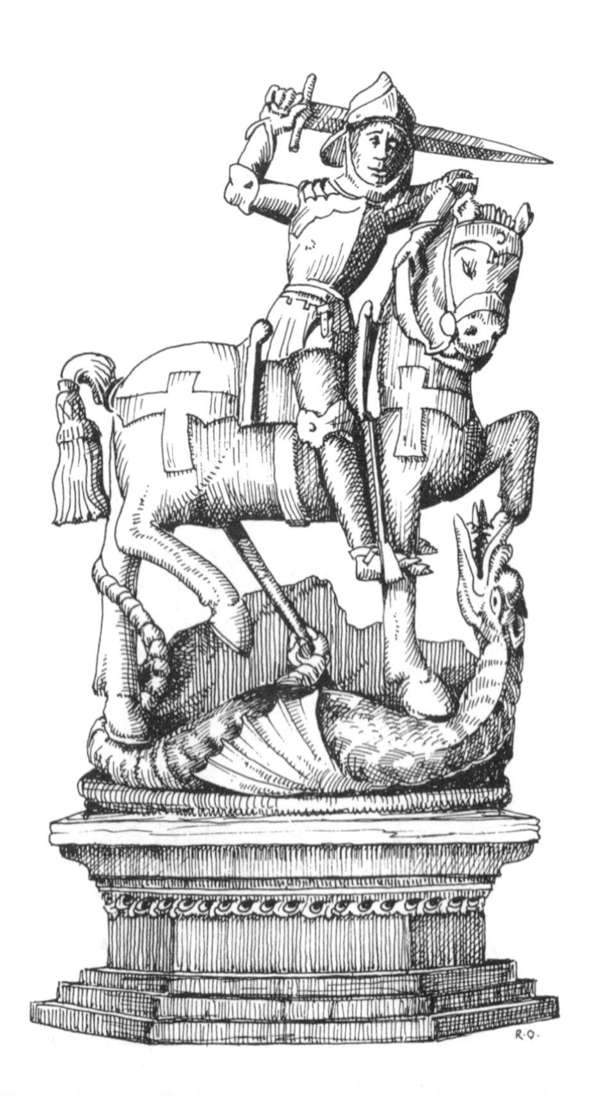

St George and the Drag

The Armoury

Approached by a newel staircase at the south-east corner of the Great Hall and the Minstrels' Gallery, behind which it lies, the Armoury is a lofty room, its open roof having 'moulded timbers and two tie-beam trusses with small curved braces and carved corbel heads'. The early **fireplace** *on the south side* (which was laid bare at a lower level during the restoration of 1925) and the **low doorway** into Caesar's Tower suggest that, at some stage, the floor has been raised. Possibly the area was divided into two rooms, one of them perhaps being the **Buttery in the Armoury,** 6*d* being paid for a key to the door in 1650. The remains of 'two long mullioned windows, one inside the other, enclosing a narrow passage', nine feet long and two feet wide could however be this **Buttery.** The inner window is part of the main structure of the rectangular timber-framed building, the outer window having been added to complete the external south wall. *To the right* are: the entry to a **blocked stairway** of nine steps which once led to a fourth storey of Caesar's Tower (added in 1731 and removed during the nineteenth century) and was rediscovered during the restoration of 1925; a fine **corbel head** with ample hair and beard, and a leaf-pattern above; the **fireplace** mentioned above; and the **entry** to the second-floor chamber of Caesar's Tower.

On the north side are two doorways from the Minstrels' Gallery either side of the range of four latticed windows of twenty-one lights; and *on the west* an enlarged latticed window – all the doors and windows probably being modern. *At the east end* is a modern half-timber screen dividing the Armoury from the new area created in 1954 when a bridge was built from the (Lord) Mayor's Parlour in the Council House across to the Armoury. New facilities include a kitchen and lavatories, both of the latter obscuring two more fine **corbel heads,** both green men, which were part of the structure of the Kitchen roof (see p68).

The city's armour (surviving pieces are displayed on the Minstrels' Gallery) was kept here, its use being intensified during the Civil War, when the Undercroft also was brought into commission as an armoury. Afterwards, the Armoury seems to have been neglected until the thorough restoration of 1925. It was badly damaged during the 1939-45 war and again restored in 1954, when it was fitted up for civic functions.

Mary Queen of Scots' Room

Plan 3

The second-floor chamber of Caesar's Tower, entered through a low (five-foot one-inch) doorway, has a brick floor and stone fireplace, beams instead of vaulting and, in addition to the square-headed window at either end, an arrow-slit in the south wall. Seventeen feet long and eleven feet wide, nine feet six inches high and with access only through the Armoury, this chamber at the top of Caesar's Tower would have provided a ready-made prison cell for Mary Queen of Scots when she was rushed south to Coventry from Tutbury in 1569 (see p15).

The Buttery (Armoury)

The Ante Room

Approached by the newel staircase (rebuilt in 1639) from the south-east corner of the Great Hall, and a right turn up some awkward steps, the Ante Room gives the appearance of the lower deck of a galleon. The floor and walls slope, and the massive transverse rafters look rather like a ship's timbers. It lies above the Gallery entrance to the Great Hall and has a view northwards across the Courtyard through a range of five two-light latticed windows with trefoil heads; there is a bench below. The room appears to be little more than an in-filling to bring the roof-line of this south side of the Courtyard up to a level with the Great Hall, the Kitchen and the Drapers' Room. There is no evidence for its use until the early-twentieth century when lack of space for corporation officials pressed it into service. It seems to have been entirely neglected except at the critical point in the nineteenth century when it had to be restored to prevent it from falling into the Courtyard. Note the massive original single **door** made of four crude vertical planks and two horizontal planks (at top and bottom), with a further strengthening on the inside.

The Kitchen

See pull out Plan 1 at the back

Although the Kitchen is not open to visitors, some description of it is essential to an understanding of St Mary's Hall, particularly as it forms part of the first hall and (like Caesar's Tower) almost certainly incorporates materials from the Norman castle of the earls of Chester. If the first Great Hall was timber-framed above a stone Undercroft, and had the normal buttery and pantry at the south end, then the present Kitchen was probably the original kitchen, built mainly of stone, but with the early-fourteenth-century **timber-framed south rooms** projecting into *the upper part of its western half. In the eastern half,* the north stone **arcade** (possibly as early as the thirteenth century, and of two bays with a central octagonal pier and a later **corbel** with an angel holding a shield) has behind it a half-timber screen probably contemporary with these south rooms, and rises behind the Gallery to roof level. The existence of the arcade suggests that the building originally extended northwards by at least twelve feet. West of the arcade, the Kitchen wall rises within the Great Hall to the level of the Minstrels' Gallery (see p51), and there is evidence of another possible **arcade** at right-angles to it, which would have run north and south across this part of the Kitchen. (The **mason's marks** recorded are similar to those found on buildings in other parts of the city.) The **small kitchen** *at the west end* (perhaps the 'jelly house' of 1581 and the larder of 1633) has an entry to the vaulted ground-floor chamber of Caesar's Tower and, *in its west wall,* a **slot perforation** which can only be explained as perhaps originally an arrow-slit.

Architecturally, the Kitchen is an enigma, containing within it features normally connected with the exterior of a building. The general impression, however, is of an earlier incomplete or ruined stone building which was finished off in 1340-42 by the insertion of the timber-framed buildings which, filling the gaps at first- and second-floor level, linked it not only with a timber-framed Great Hall but also with all three floors of Caesar's Tower.

At its full height, the Kitchen was a lofty, open room with its roof (thought to be of a later date) retaining 'tie-beams with small curved braces resting on carved head-stops', but the central louvre it once had has gone. 'There are four **hearths** in arched recesses incorporated in the south and east walls, the flues being carried up between the windows'. In the interests of hygiene however, the walls of the Kitchen are now lined with formica, and a new ceiling at a lower level was inserted in 1954 to allow for the bridge from the Council House to the Armoury and the new facilities there. It is therefore no longer possible to see many of the features described above. There is an external door in the south wall;

The Kitchen

to the west a doorway leads to the smaller kitchen and in the north wall a staircase leads up to the Great Hall, emerging between the Old Council Chamber and the Prince's Chamber; two staircases lead down on this side to the Undercroft, one from the main Kitchen and one (now blocked) from the smaller kitchen; at the east end of the north side is an exit by the scullery to the Courtyard.

The Kitchen, in its hey-day, was well supplied with cooking utensils, pantries and cupboards, racks, spits (fifteen in 1619), a large dripping pan and cauldrons. New ranges were installed in 1617 when James I visited Coventry, and repairs were frequently carried out throughout the centuries.

The 14th century kitchen

Appendix

List of the pictures hanging in St Mary's Hall in 1948 and now in the Herbert Art Gallery

**Although it is hoped that most of the pictures listed will in due course be returned to St Mary's Hall, those marked with an asterisk, together with Giordano's Bacchus and Ariadne (see p52), will remain in the Art Gallery*

Alleged portrait of *Henry V*
(found to be a nineteenth-century work which may, or may not, be a copy), the original having existed in St Mary's Hall in 1474

*Alleged portrait of *Mary Tudor*
(formerly said to be after Antonio Moro). Although the painting is of exquisite workmanship, the subject and the artist are (alike) unidentified

Queen Elizabeth I
(closely connected with an engraving by William Rogers), purchased in 1629 probably as the first of a series of royal portraits

James I
(artist unknown, but perhaps copied from the portrait by Daniel Mytens in the National Portrait Gallery), purchased in 1626 and either re-purchased or restored in 1661

Charles I
(artist unknown – a poor copy of an unidentified original), purchased in 1626 and either re-purchased or restored in 1661

Queen Mary II
(artist unknown), purchased in London in 1691

Queen Anne
(artist unknown)

George II
(artist unknown), painted as Prince of Wales

George III
*(by Sir Thomas Lawrence), presented to the city by its two members of parliament, Lord Eardley and J Wilmot Esq, in 1792

Lady Godiva
*(artist unknown) perhaps Flemish), purchased in 1586, of unusual interest: the horse well-painted, the buildings of Renaissance style, a gilded Coventry Cross, and a figure at a window on the right. The staff of the Art Gallery and Museum suggest that this may be a self-portrait by the artist and that it may have been one of the sources of the Peeping Tom story. In 1681, 'Mr Ellis the Limner' made a copy which may be returned to St Mary's Hall in due course

Sir Thomas White
1492-1567 (artist unknown), hung in St Mary's Hall in 1593. Founded a charity in Coventry and four other towns

Christopher Davenport
d 1629 (artist unknown). Mayor 1602; founded a charity in Coventry

Simon Norton
d 1641 (artist unknown). Mayor 1633; founded a charity in Coventry

**Samuel Baker*
d 1695 (artist unknown). Founded a charity school in Coventry in 1690

**John Neale* of Allesley 1687-1746 (artist unknown). MP for Coventry 1722-41. Neale presented the portrait (which was thought in 1948 to be of George I) to the City Council

Sir Skears Rew
(artist unknown). Mayor 1815 and 1816

Alderman Samuel Whitwell
(painted by public subscription for presentation to Mr Whitwell, 1830, and presented to the City Council, 1888). Mayor 1800-1 and 1828-30

A portrait of *Thomas Wheatley* (fl 1563 and founded Bablake School), was in existence in St Mary's Hall in 1597 and again in 1719, but had disappeared by 1946

Bibliography

Primary Sources

Published Editions

The Coventry Leet Book... ed M D Harris (Early English Text Soc: Orig Ser Nos 134-5, 138, 146, 1907-13)

The Register of the Guild of the Holy Trinity... ed M D Harris (Dugdale Soc: Publns xiii, 1935)

Coventry Record Office

The records of the Guild of the Holy Trinity ii ed G Templeman (Dugdale Soc: Publns xix, 1944)

Chamberlains' Accounts (A7)

Book of Payments Out (A16)

Treasurer's Accounts (A36)

Council Minute Books (A14)

Committee Minute Books Estates Com (A174 etc)

Accounts of the Guild and Chantry Lands (A21)

City Annals (A28, 37, 43, 48)

Robert Beake's Diary (A105)

History of the Guilds of the City of Coventry (A165)

Deeds; Bills and Receipts; Correspondence

St Mary's Hall: Report on the recent excavations, by Alderman Andrews, 1900

St Mary's Hall: Report on the north wall, by H T Jackson, 1930

Official programme for the unveiling of the new windows presented to the city by William Coker Iliffe Esq, 28 October 1930

Official programme for the re-opening of the Old Council Chamber at St Mary's Hall, 27 May 1936

Shakespeare Birthplace Trust MS DR/18/31/3

Birmingham Reference Library MSS 87,736; 115,915; 273,978

Public Record Office E164/21 *and* a translation of a portion of it: *The Pittancer's rental 1410-11* (University of Birmingham, Dept of Extramural Studies, 1973); C66/235

British Library Harl MSS 539; 6,388; 7,017; Duke of Portland MSS: Harley Papers xxxiv (BM Loan 29/205)

Secondary Works

Dugdale, *Sir* William, *Warwickshire* 1st edn (1656); 2nd edn (1730)

Pennant, Thomas, *The journey from Chester to London* (London, 1811)

Warwickshire:... from the elaborate work of Sir William Dugdale and other later authorities (Coventry, 1817)

Cooke, GA, *Topographical and statistical description of the county of Warwick* (London, [*c* 1816-20])

[Sharp, Thomas], *The Coventry Guide* (Coventry, 1824)

Reader, William, *New Coventry Guide* (Coventry, [*c* 1824-26])

Reader, William, *A Guide to St Mary's Hall, Coventry,* 2nd edn (1827)

Sharp, Thomas, *A concise history of Coventry*... new edn [issued in parts *c* 1843+]

Poole, Benjamin, *Coventry: its history and antiquities*... illustrns by W Fred Taunton (London and Coventry, 1870)

Sharp, Thomas, *Illustrative papers on the history and antiquities of the city of Coventry* ed W G Fretton (Coventry, 1871)

Lambert, *Major* George, *Cocked Hats at Coventry* (London, 1888)

Fretton, W G, *Memorials of St Mary's Hall, Coventry* (1891) – kindly lent to the author by Mr and Mrs D Watson

Rackham, Bernard, 'Glass-paintings of Coventry and its neighbourhood' (Walpole Soc: 19th vol for 1930-31, 1931)

Millar, Oliver, *Tudor, Stuart and early Georgian pictures in the collection of Her Majesty The Queen* (London, 1963)

Garlick, Kenneth, *comp* 'A catalogue of the paintings, drawings and pastels of Sir Thomas Lawrence' (Walpole Soc: 39th vol for 1962-64, 1964)

Stone, Lawrence, *Sculpture in Britain: the middle ages* (Pelican History of Art, 1955)

Warwickshire, by Nikolaus Pevsner and Alexandra Wedgwood (The Buildings of England, 1966)

The City of Coventry and Borough of Warwick (Victoria History of the County of Warwick viii, 1969)

Notes on the Council House and St Mary's Hall (Coventry: Public Relations Dept, 1968)

Notes

Designed by the Graphic and Visual Aids Division of the Department of Architecture and Planning GVA 44 JSG 81

Notes

Plan 1
Ground Floor
Rooms

Plan 2
First Floor
Rooms